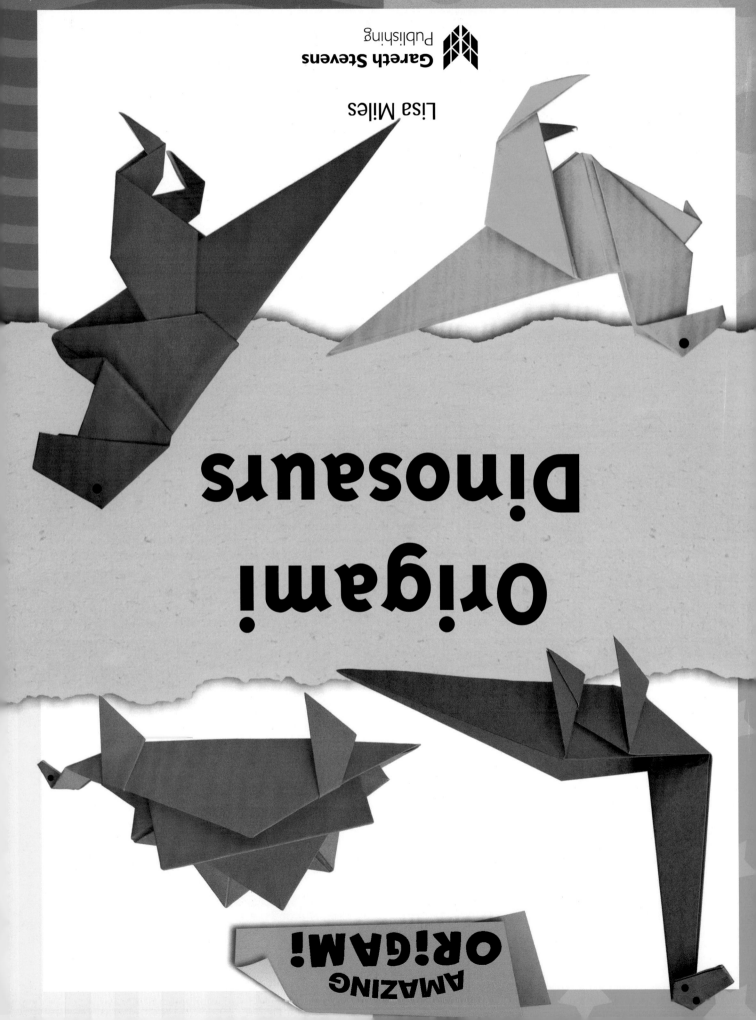

Origami Dinosaurs

Lisa Miles

Gareth Stevens Publishing

AMAZING ORIGAMI

Please visit our website, www.garethstevens.com. For a free color catalog of all our high-quality books, call toll free 1-800-542-2595 or fax 1-877-542-2596.

Library of Congress Cataloging-in-Publication Data

Miles, Lisa.
   Origami dinosaurs / Lisa Miles.
      pages   cm. – (Amazing origami)
   Includes index.
   ISBN 978-1-4339-9649-8 (pbk.)
   ISBN 978-1-4339-9650-4 (6-pack)
   ISBN 978-1-4339-9648-1 (library binding)
   1. Origami–Juvenile literature. 2. Dinosaurs–Juvenile literature.   I. Title.
TT872.5.M553 2013
736'.982–dc23
                                                        2012050336

First Edition

Published in 2014 by
Gareth Stevens Publishing
111 East 14th Street, Suite 349
New York, NY 10003

Copyright © 2014 Arcturus Publishing

Models and photography: Belinda Webster and Michael Wiles
Text: Lisa Miles
Design: Emma Randall
Editors: Anna Brett, Becca Clunes, and Joe Harris
Animal photography: Shutterstock

Printed in the United States of America

CPSIA compliance information: Batch #CS13GS: For further information contact Gareth Stevens, New York, New York at 1-800-542-2595.

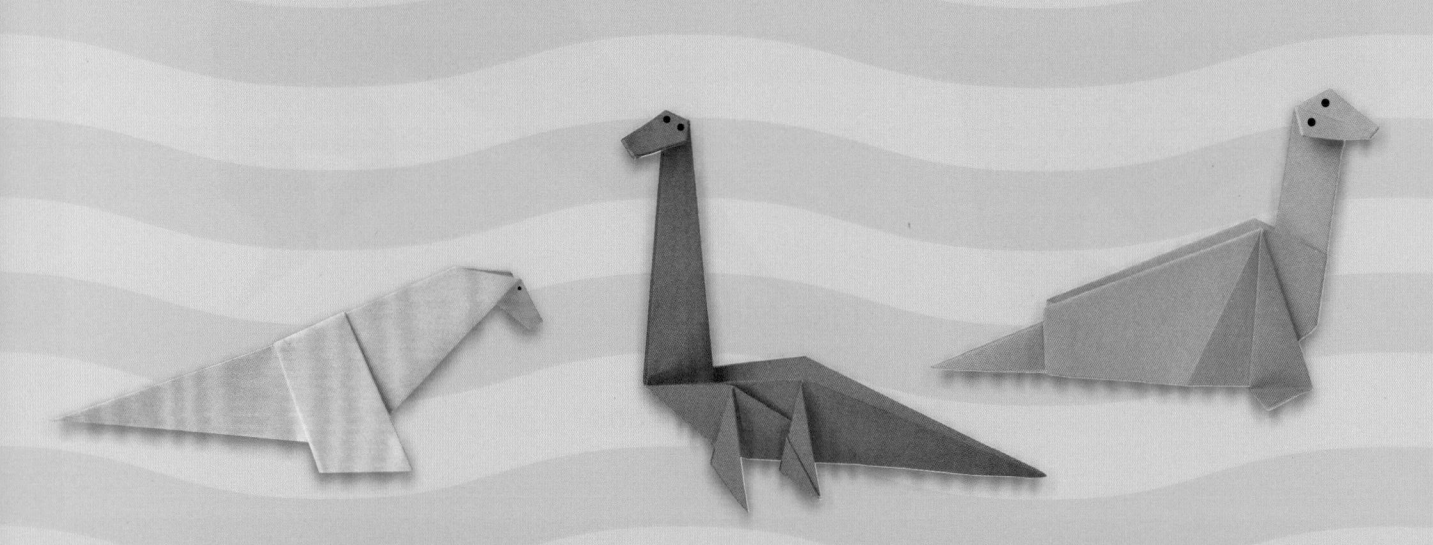

Contents

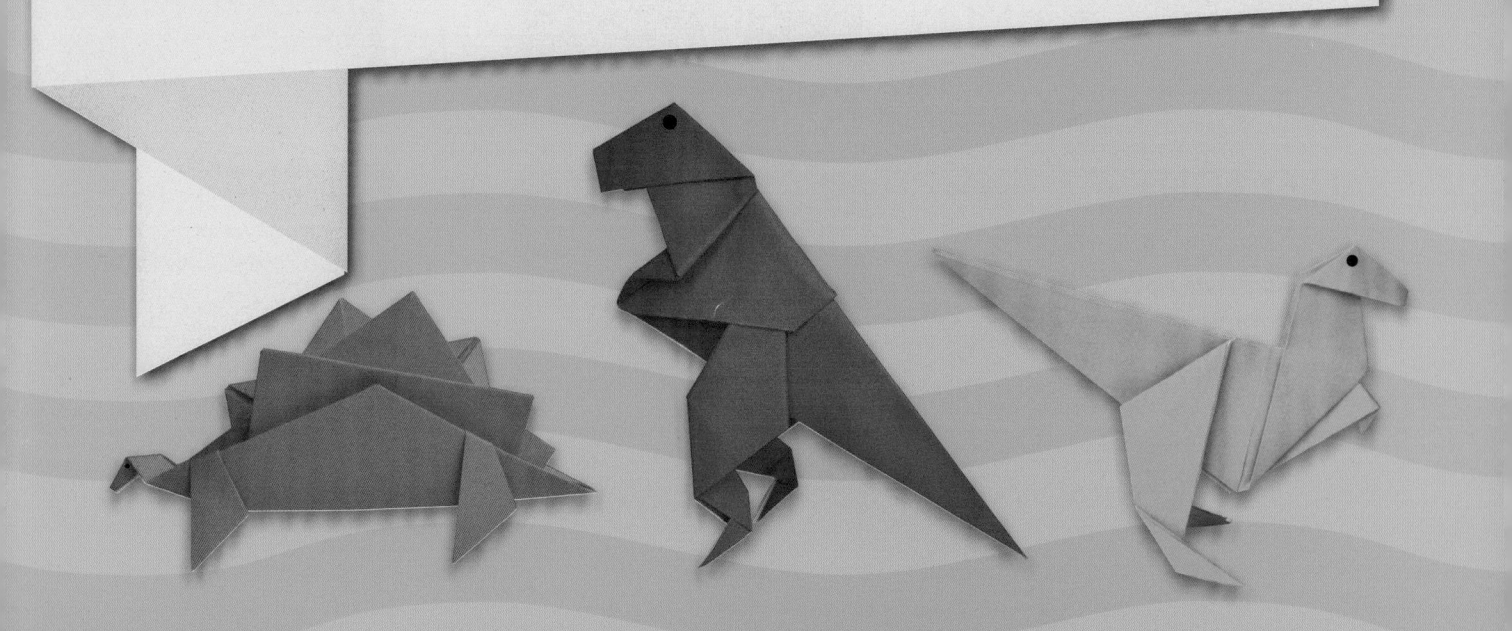

Basic Folds

Origami has been popular in Japan for hundreds of years and is now loved all around the world. You can make great origami models with just one sheet of paper... and this book shows you how!

The paper used in origami is thin but strong, so that it can be folded many times. It is usually colored on one side. You can also use ordinary scrap paper, but make sure it's not too thick.

Origami models often share the same folds and basic designs, known as "bases." This introduction explains some of the folds and bases that you will need for the projects in this book. When making the models, follow the key below to find out what the lines and arrows mean. And always crease well!

KEY

valley fold - - - - - - - - - - - - - - - -

mountain fold ....

step fold (mountain and valley fold next to each other)

direction to move paper

push ◀

MOUNTAIN FOLD

To make a mountain fold, fold the paper so that the crease is pointing up toward you, like a mountain.

VALLEY FOLD

To make a valley fold, fold the paper the other way, so that the crease is pointing away from you, like a valley.

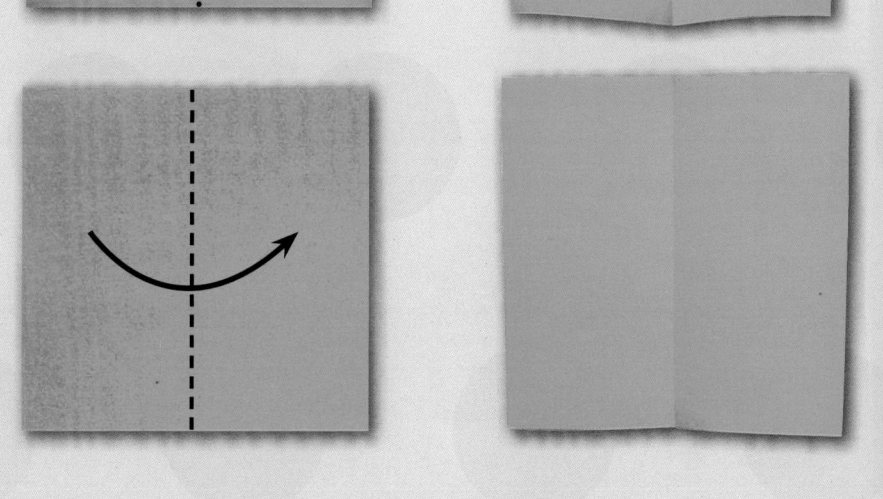

INSIDE REVERSE FOLD

An inside reverse fold is useful if you want to make a nose or a tail, or if you want to flatten the shape of another part of an origami model.

① Practice by first folding a piece of paper diagonally in half. Make a valley fold on one point and crease.

② It's important to make sure that the paper is creased well. Run your finger over the crease two or three times.

③ Unfold and open up the corner slightly. Refold the crease nearest to you into a mountain fold.

Open

④ Open up the paper a little more and then tuck the tip of the point inside. Close the paper. This is the view from the underside of the paper.

⑤ Flatten the paper. You now have an inside reverse fold.

OUTSIDE REVERSE FOLD

An outside reverse fold is useful if you want to make a head, beak, foot, or another part of your model that sticks out.

① Practice by first folding a piece of paper diagonally in half. Make a valley fold on one point and crease.

② It's important to make sure that the paper is creased well. Run your finger over the crease two or three times.

③ Unfold and open up the corner slightly. Refold the crease furthest away from you into a valley fold.

Open

④ Open up the paper a little more and start to turn the corner inside out. Then close the paper when the fold begins to turn.

⑤ You now have an outside reverse fold. You can either flatten the paper or leave it rounded out.

Bases

KITE BASE

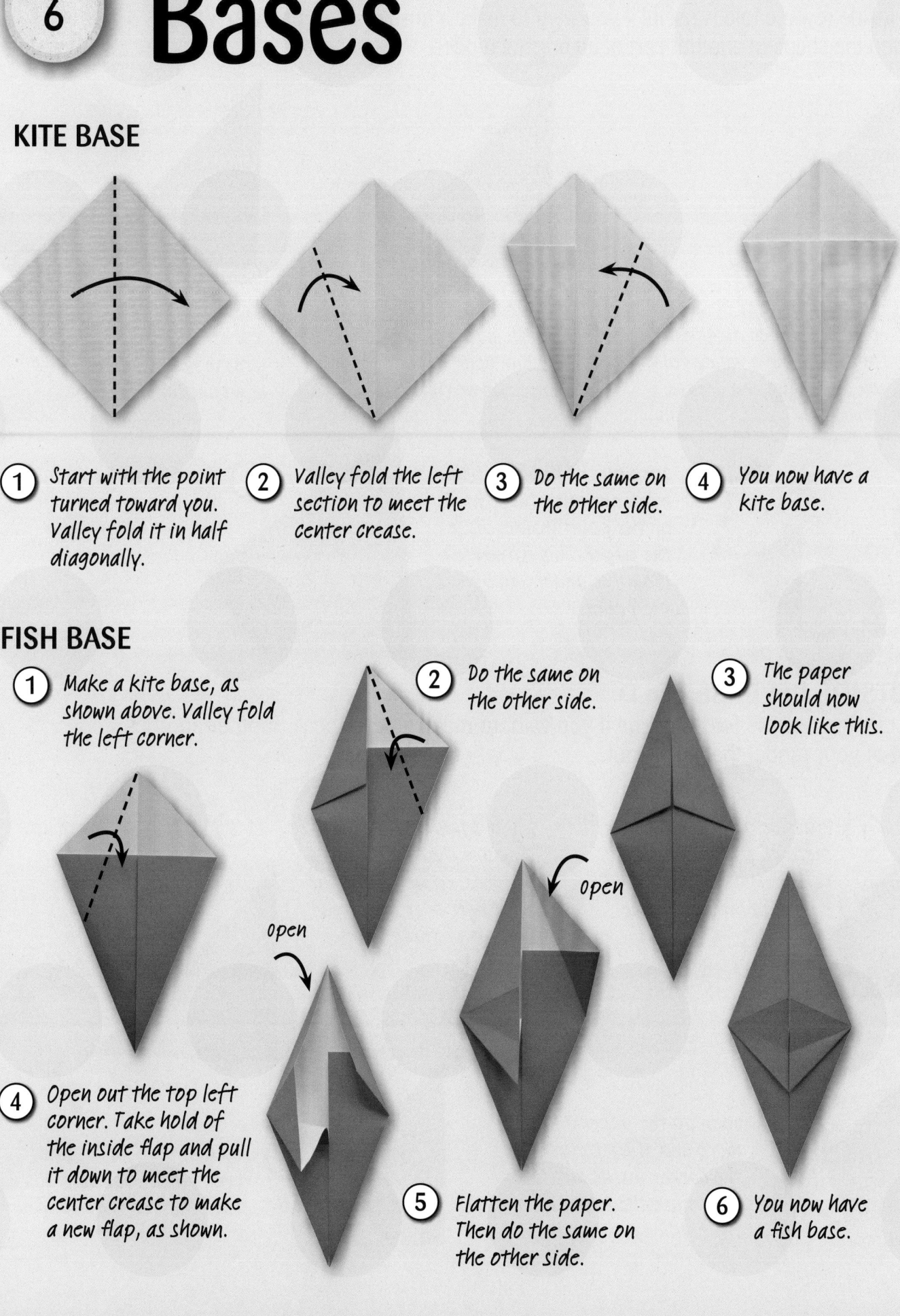

① Start with the point turned toward you. Valley fold it in half diagonally.

② Valley fold the left section to meet the center crease.

③ Do the same on the other side.

④ You now have a kite base.

FISH BASE

① Make a kite base, as shown above. Valley fold the left corner.

② Do the same on the other side.

③ The paper should now look like this.

open

open

④ Open out the top left corner. Take hold of the inside flap and pull it down to meet the center crease to make a new flap, as shown.

⑤ Flatten the paper. Then do the same on the other side.

⑥ You now have a fish base.

BIRD BASE

1 Start with a corner turned towards you. Mountain fold diagonally both ways.

2 Valley fold along the horizontal and vertical lines.

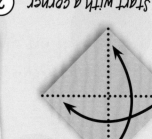

3 Hold the paper by opposite diagonal corners. Push the two corners together so that the shape begins to collapse.

push   push

4 The paper should collapse into a square shape. Turn the open end to face you. Then valley fold the top left flap to the center crease.

5 Do the same on the other side.

6 Valley fold the top triangle.

7 Unfold the top and sides and you have the shape shown here.

8 Take the bottom corner and begin to open out the upper flap by gently pulling upwards.

Pull

9 The paper should open like a bird's beak. Open out the flap as far as it will go.

10 Flatten the paper so that you now have this shape. Turn the paper over.

11 The paper should now look like this. Repeat steps 4 through 10 on this side.

12 You now have a bird base. The two flaps at the bottom are separated by an open slit.

Compsognathus

Compsognathus was a small, fast-moving dinosaur about the size of a turkey. It ran around on its back legs, using its long tail for balance.

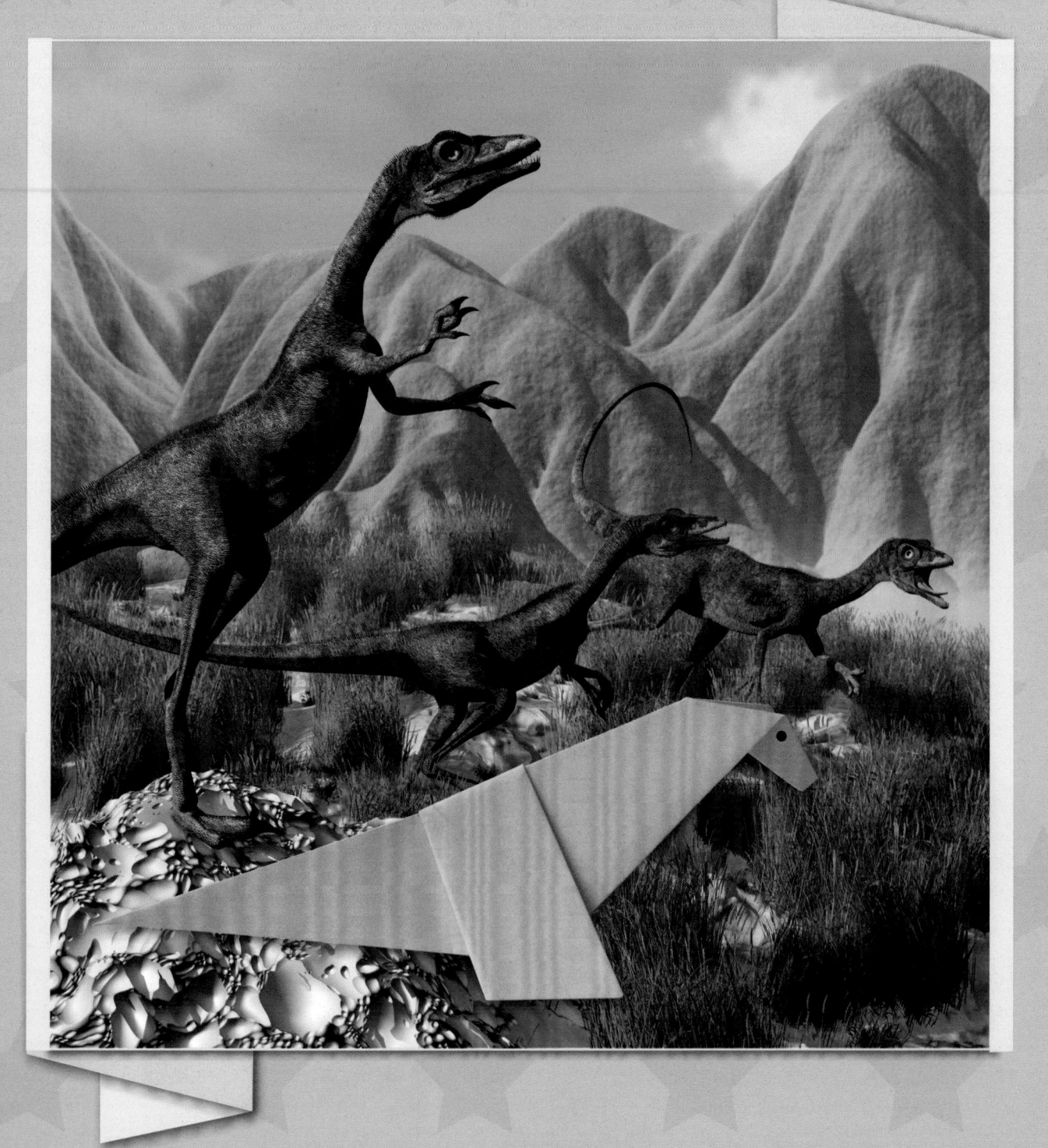

Start with
a kite
base

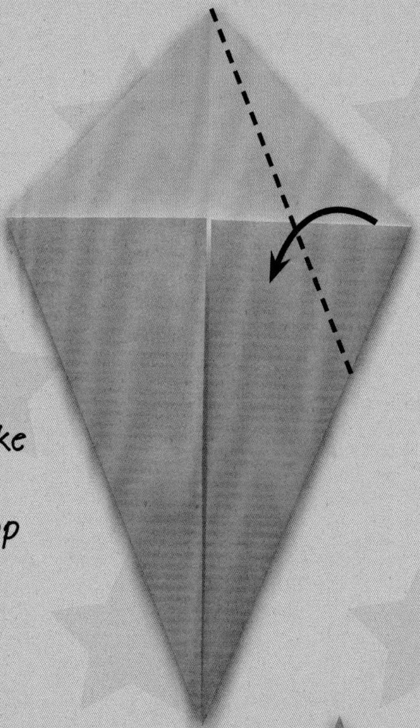

1 Find out how to make
a kite base on page
6. Valley fold the top
right corner.

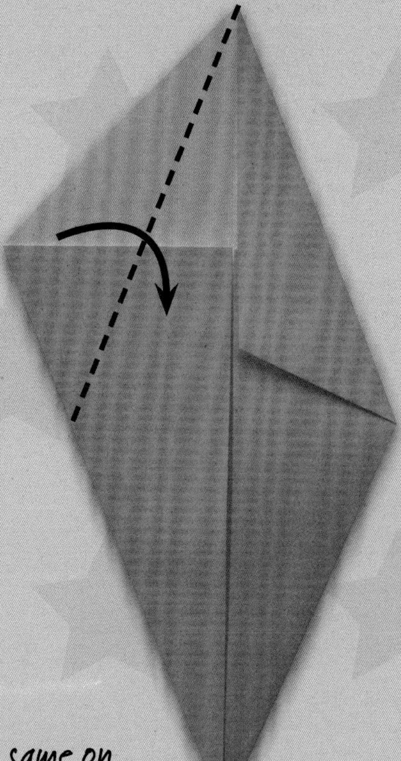

2 Do the same on
the other side.

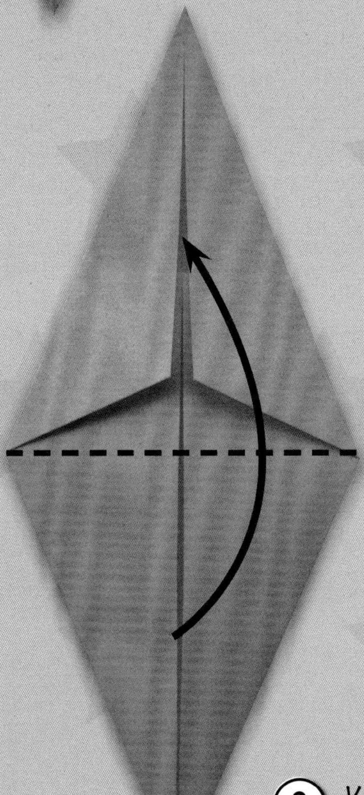

3 Valley fold in half,
from bottom to top.

6 Valley fold the paper in half from left to right.

4 Valley fold the top section down.

5 Valley fold the top flap back up.

7 Turn the paper around to the position shown here. Mountain fold the left point.

8 Unfold, then make an inside reverse fold to create the head.

9 Tuck the tip of the nose in to make it blunt.

10 Your origami Compsognathus is finished and ready to run! Why not make some friends for it?

Diplodocus

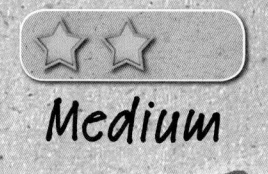

Medium

Diplodocus was a huge plant-eating dinosaur. It may have used its long, powerful tail like a whip to strike at its enemies.

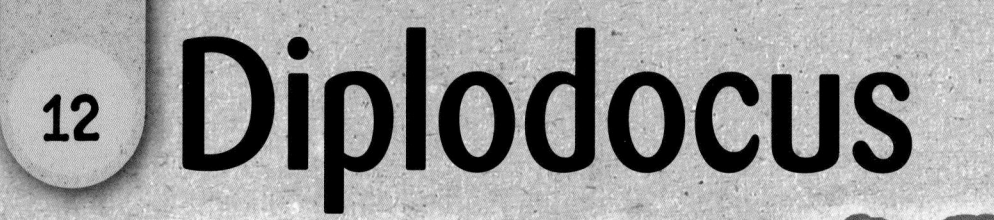

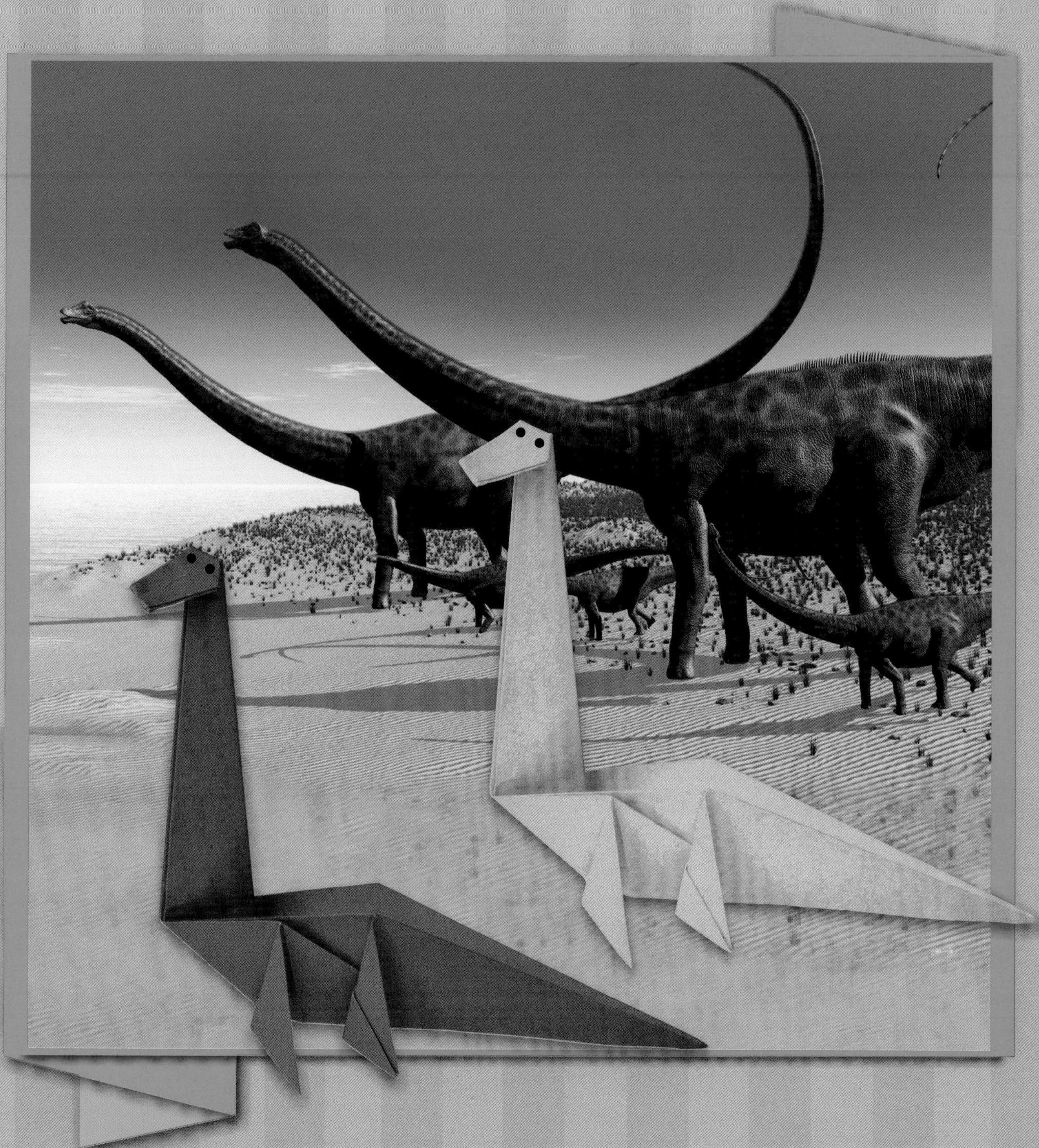

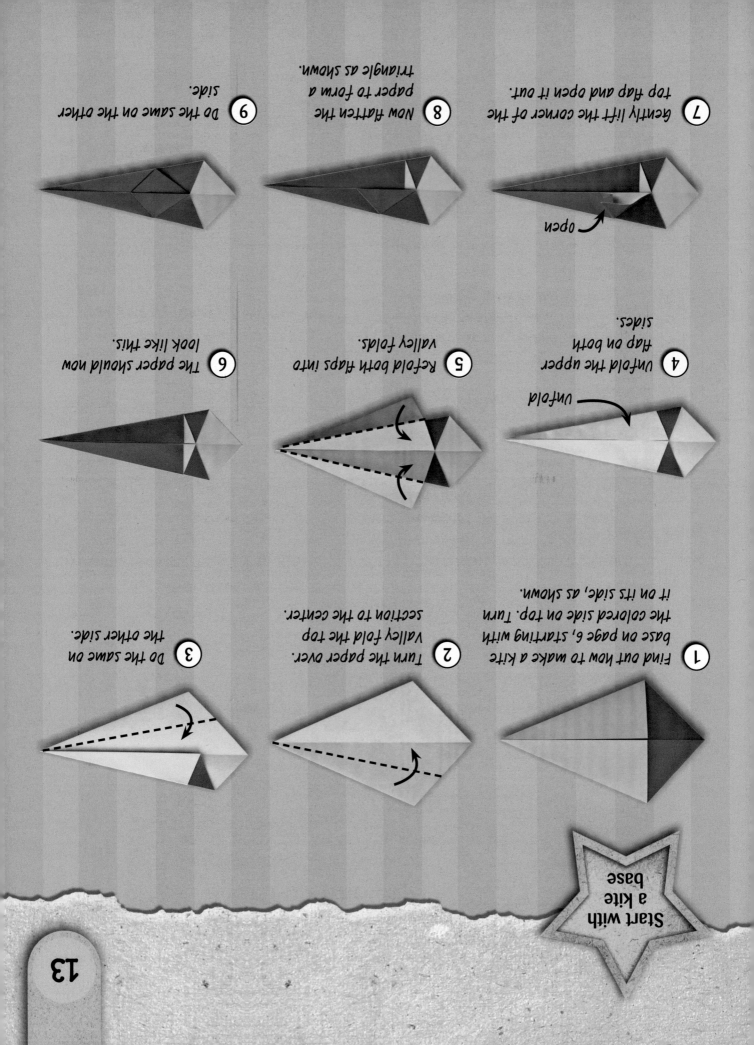

Start with a kite base

1 Find out how to make a kite base on page 6, starting with the colored side on top. Turn it on its side, as shown.

2 Turn the paper over. Valley fold the top section to the center.

3 Do the same on the other side.

4 Unfold the upper flap on both sides.

unfold

5 Refold both flaps into valley folds.

6 The paper should now look like this.

7 Gently lift the corner of the top flap and open it out.

open

8 Now flatten the paper to form a triangle as shown.

9 Do the same on the other side.

Did You Know?

Diplodocus was a truly enormous animal. From head to tail, it was about 148 feet (45 m) long.

open

10 Gently open out the left corner.

11 Flatten the paper into a triangle as shown, so that it slightly overlaps the triangle you made in step 8.

12 Do the same on the other side. Mountain fold in half, so that the bottom folds behind the top.

13 The flaps should point to the right. Fold the two flaps back to form the legs. Do the same on both sides.

14 Valley fold the right point so that it goes straight up.

15 Unfold, then make an inside reverse fold to create the neck.

16 Flatten the paper.

17 Mountain fold the right point.

18 Unfold, then make an inside reverse fold to create the head.

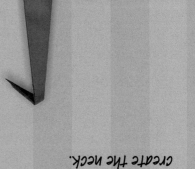

19 Flatten the head and angle it a little bit. Tuck in the tip of the nose to make it blunt.

20 Stand up your cute origami diplodocus—but watch out for that whipping tail!

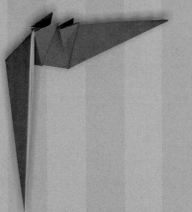

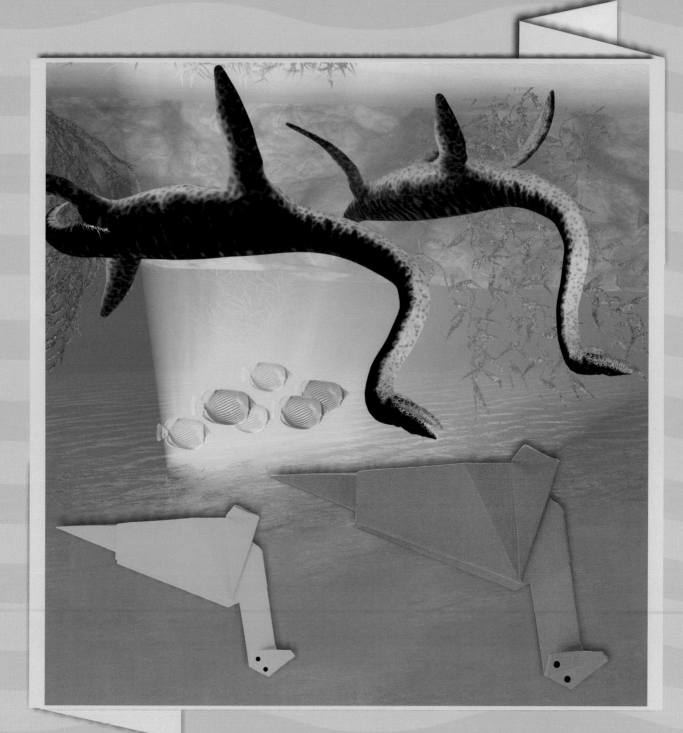

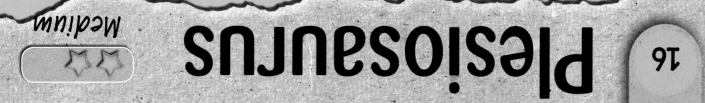

When dinosaurs were roaming Earth, giant long-necked reptiles called plesiosaurs swam in the oceans. This one is called Plesiosaurus.

Plesiosaurus

Start with a fish base

1 Find out how to make a fish base on page 6. With the flaps pointing to the left, mountain fold in half.

2 Valley fold the top flap in to the center. Then do the same on the other side.

3 Valley fold the left point up.

4 Unfold, then make an inside reverse fold to create the neck. Make the neck stand straight up.

5 Mountain fold the upper flap of the neck inside itself, so that it becomes a narrow strip.

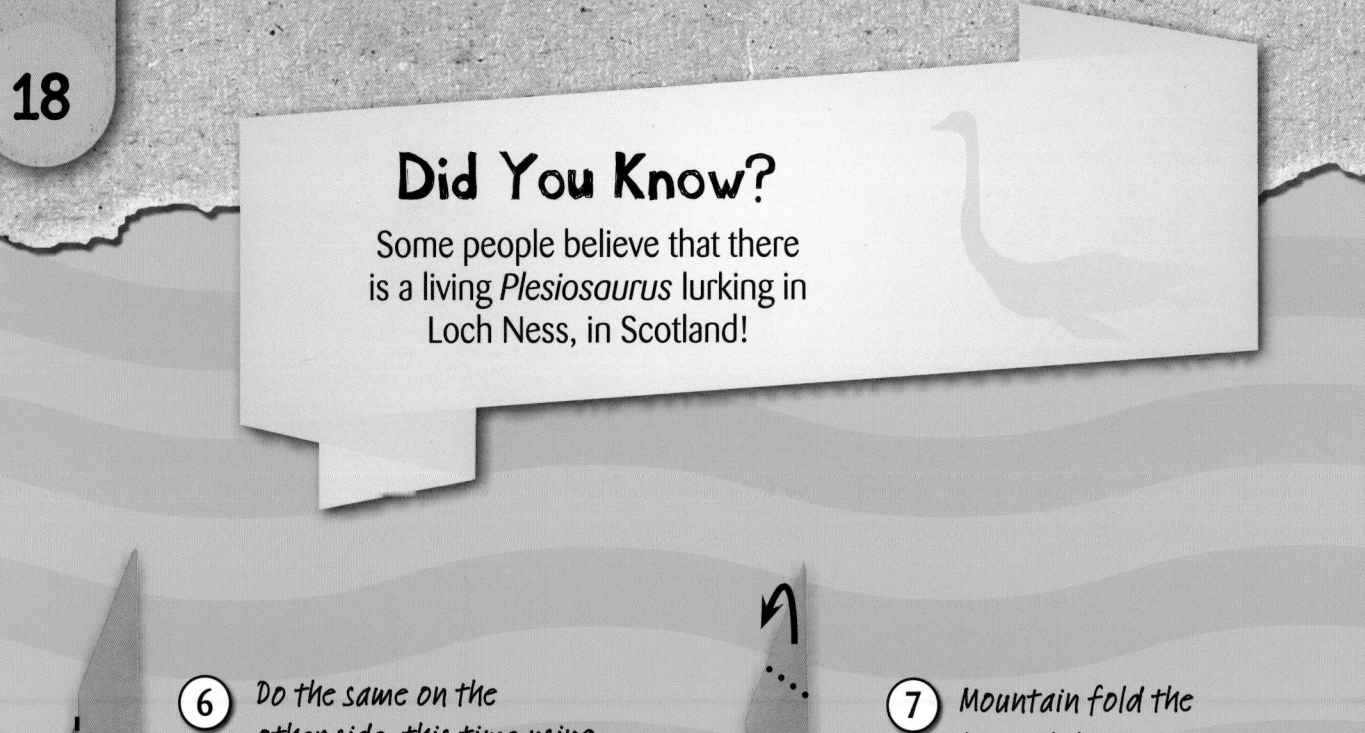

Did You Know?
Some people believe that there is a living *Plesiosaurus* lurking in Loch Ness, in Scotland!

⑥ Do the same on the other side, this time using a valley fold.

⑦ Mountain fold the top point.

⑧ Unfold, then make an inside reverse fold to create the head. Flatten it and angle it.

⑨ Tuck in the end of the nose. Then mountain fold and valley fold the tail to make a step fold.

10 Unfold, then tuck the tail in and then out again along the fold lines.

11 Valley fold the bottom point.

12 Do the same on the other side to create two flippers.

13 Balance the Plesiosaurus on its flippers. And now you have an origami prehistoric sea monster!

Allosaurus

Allosaurus was much like its more famous cousin, *T. rex*. Although it wasn't quite as big in length or height, it was still a fearsome fighter!

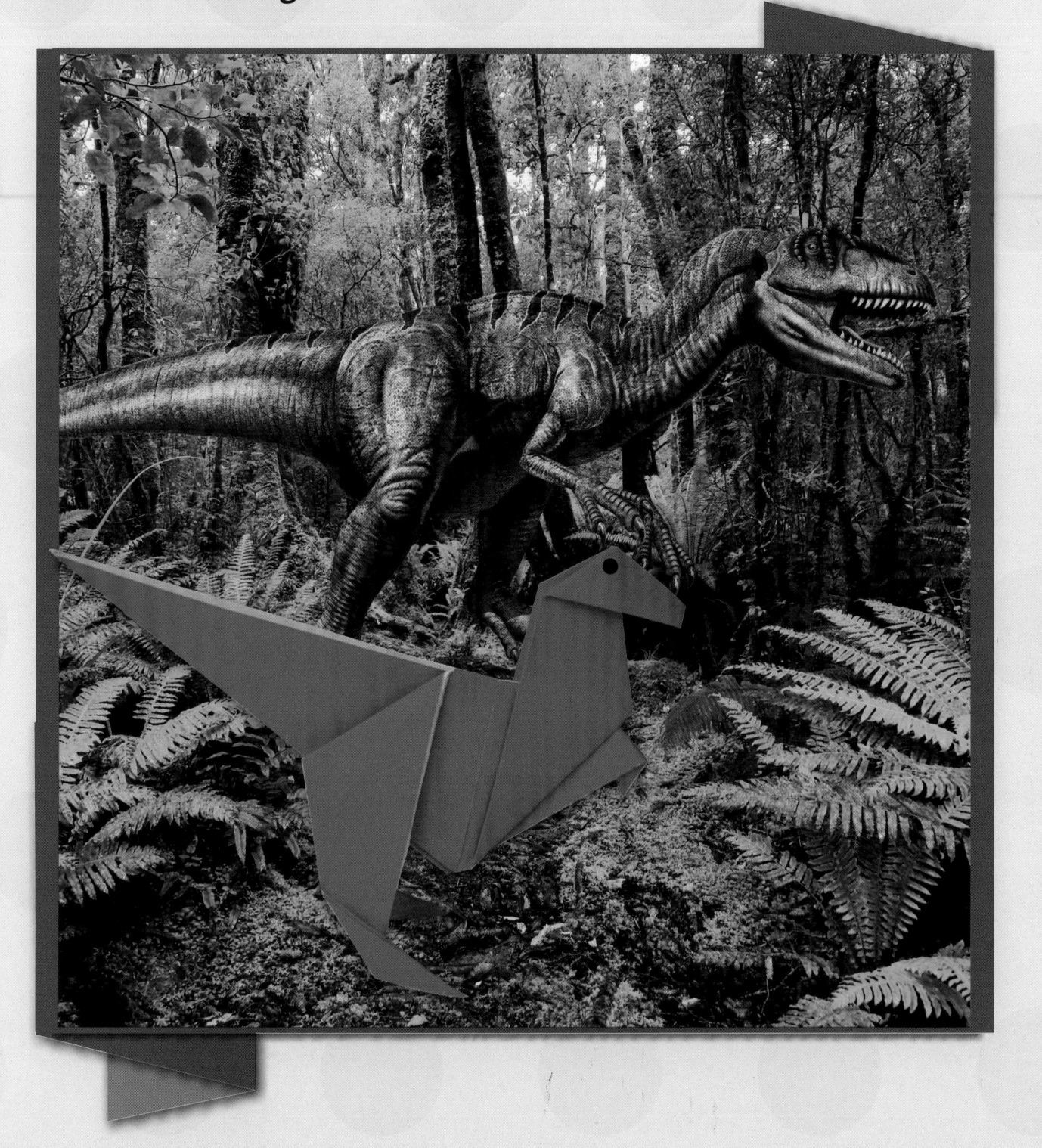

Start with a bird base

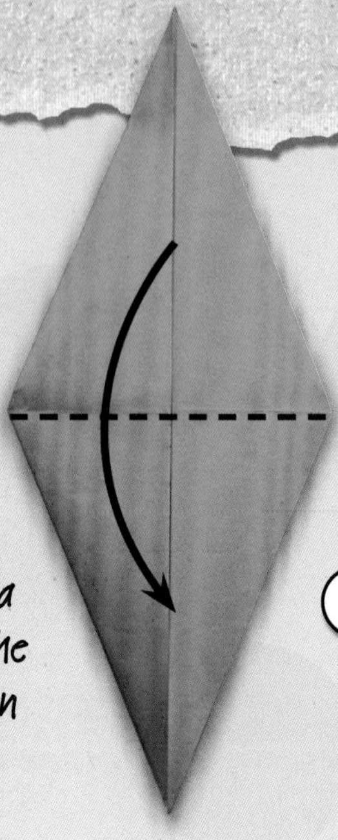

1 Find out how to make a bird base on page 7. The two flaps with the open slit point down. Valley fold the front flap.

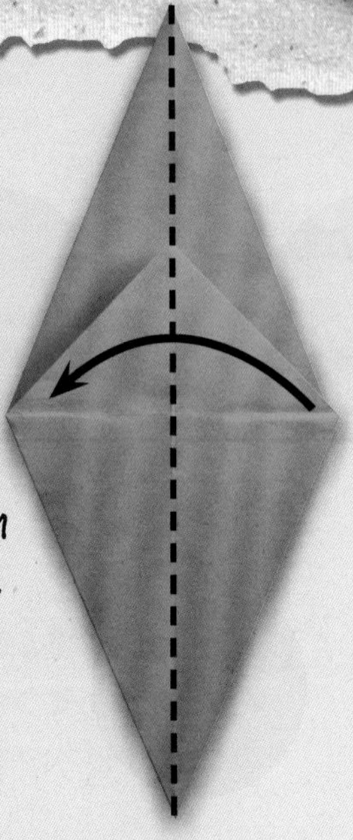

2 Valley fold the paper in half from right to left. Turn it around so that the open flaps are on the right.

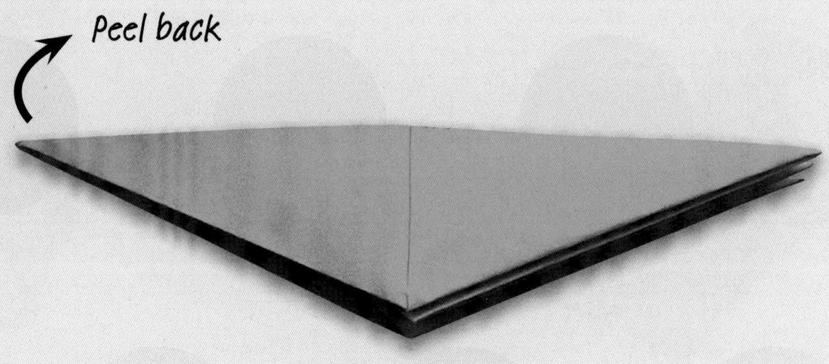

3 Peel back the left flap to reveal the triangle underneath, as shown in step 4.

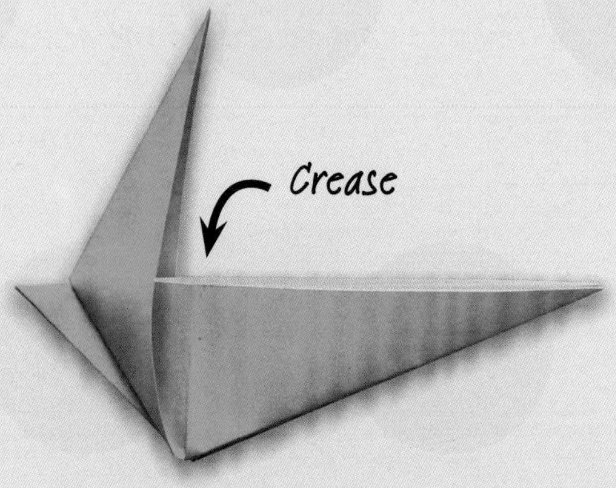

Peel back

4 The edge of the upright piece should meet the crease on the body. Flatten the paper.

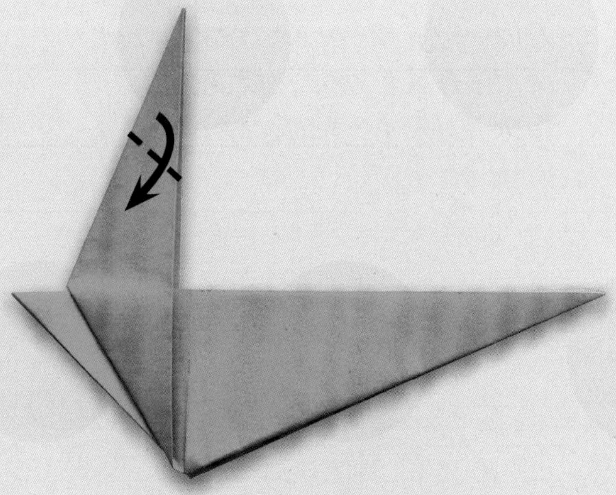

Crease

5 Valley fold the top point.

6 Unfold, then make an inside reverse fold to create the arms.

8 Valley fold the point sticking out of the front. Your fold should tuck inside the neck cavity just a little bit.

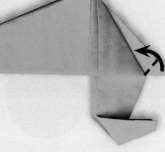

7 Tuck the tip of the nose inside to make it blunt.

9 Unfold, then make an outside reverse fold to create the head.

13 Your fierce origami Allosaurus should now balance on its feet. Watch out, dinosaurs!

12 Do the same on the other side.

11 Valley fold the bottom tip of the leg to create a foot.

10 Valley fold the top flap down to create a leg. Do the same on the other side.

24 Stegosaurus

☆☆ Medium

Stegosaurus had two rows of spiky plates running along its back. They were used to help keep the dinosaur warm. *Stegosaurus* turned its side towards the sun to warm up.

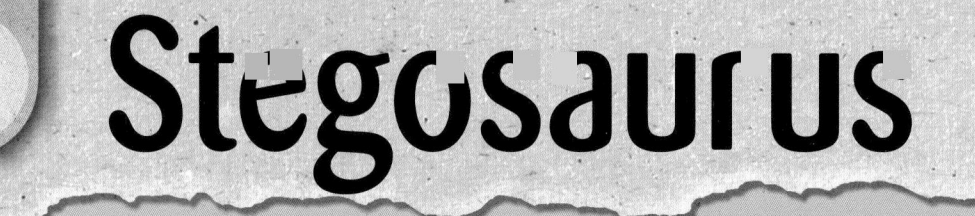

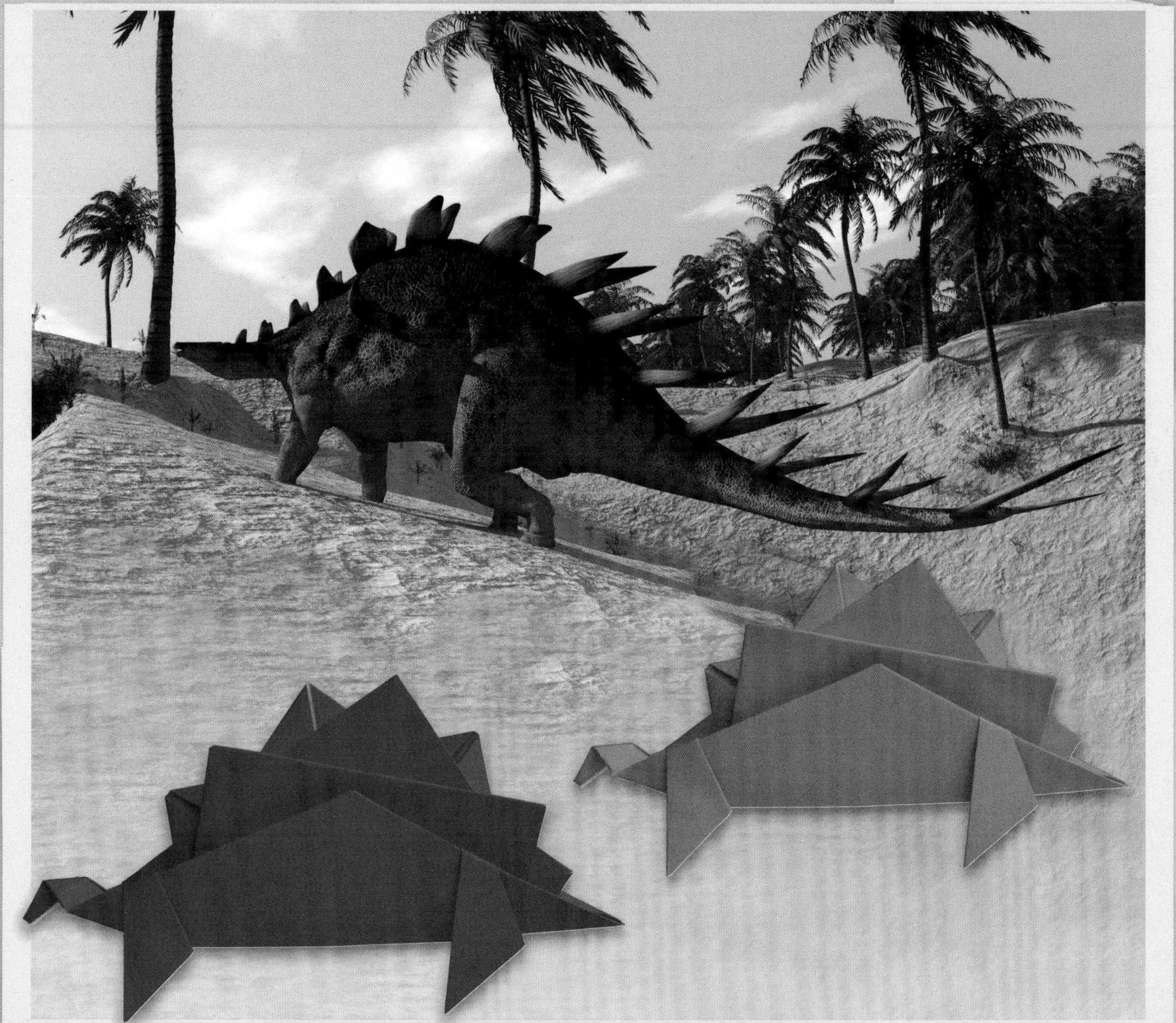

MAKE THE HEAD AND BODY

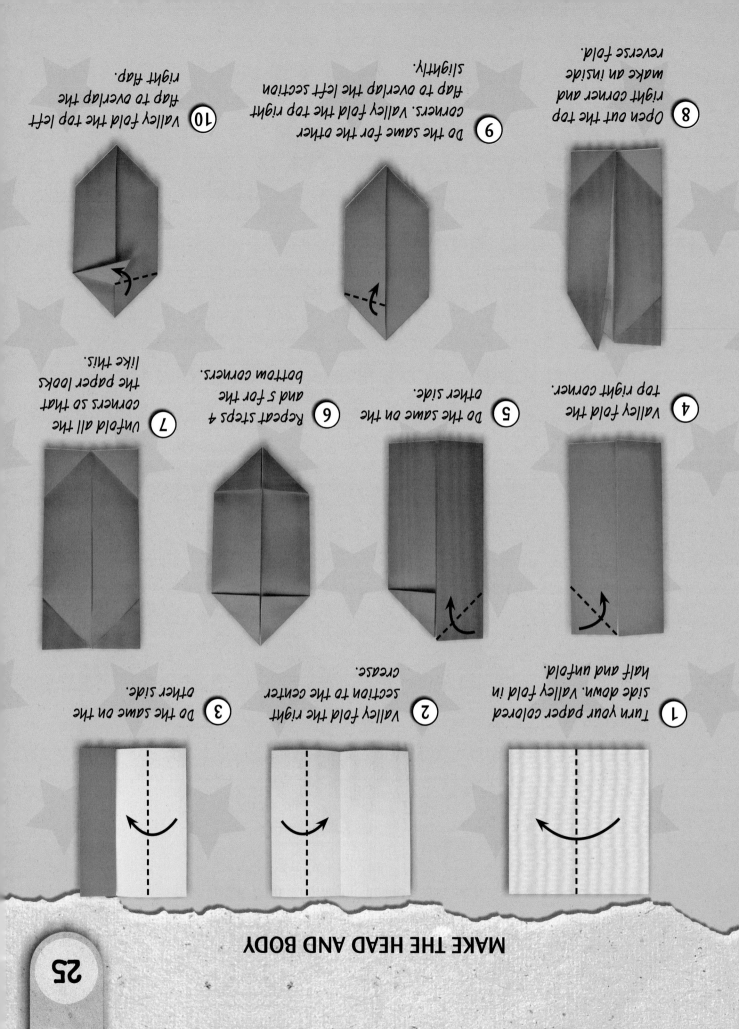

1 Turn your paper colored side down. Valley fold in half and unfold.

2 Valley fold the right section to the center crease.

3 Do the same on the other side.

4 Valley fold the top right corner.

5 Do the same on the other side.

6 Repeat steps 4 and 5 for the bottom corners.

7 Unfold all the corners so that the paper looks like this.

8 Open out the top right corner and make an inside reverse fold.

9 Do the same for the other corners. Valley fold the top right flap to overlap the left section slightly.

10 Valley fold the top left flap to overlap the right flap.

Did You Know?

Stegosaurus had four long spikes at the end of its tail. It could swing its tail to scare away meat-eating dinosaurs.

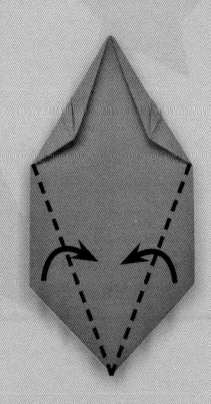

11 Repeat steps 9 and 10 for the bottom flaps.

12 The paper should now look like this. Turn the paper over.

13 Valley fold the top edges.

14 Valley fold the right and left corners to meet in the center.

15 Valley fold the paper in half from right to left.

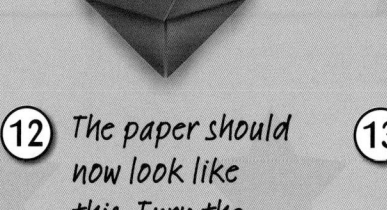

16 Turn the paper as shown, so the feet are pointing down. Mountain fold the left point.

17 Unfold, then make an inside reverse fold to create the neck.

18 Mountain fold the left point.

19 Now make an outside reverse fold to create the head. Tuck in the tip of the nose to make it blunt.

1 Start with your paper colored side down. Valley fold into quarters.

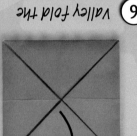

2 Unfold, then valley fold the top right corner into the center.

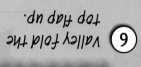

3 Do the same for the other three corners.

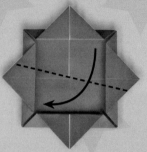

4 Valley fold the right corner into the center.

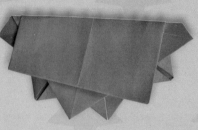

5 Do the same for the other corners.

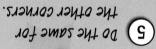

6 Valley fold the top flap up.

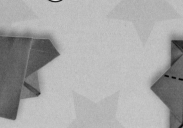

7 Do the same for the other flaps.

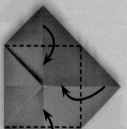

8 Valley fold the bottom section of the paper up at an angle, as shown, so that the triangles form an arc.

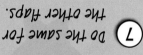

9 The paper should now look like this. This is the spiky back of the Stegosaurus.

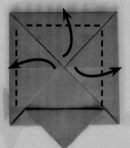

10 Slot the Stegosaurus's back into the body. Now you have one spiky origami dinosaur!

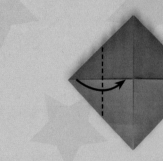

T. rex

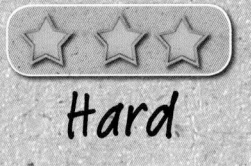

Tyrannosaurus rex, or *T. rex* for short, was a fierce meat eater with a big head and sharp teeth. Its name means "tyrant lizard king"!

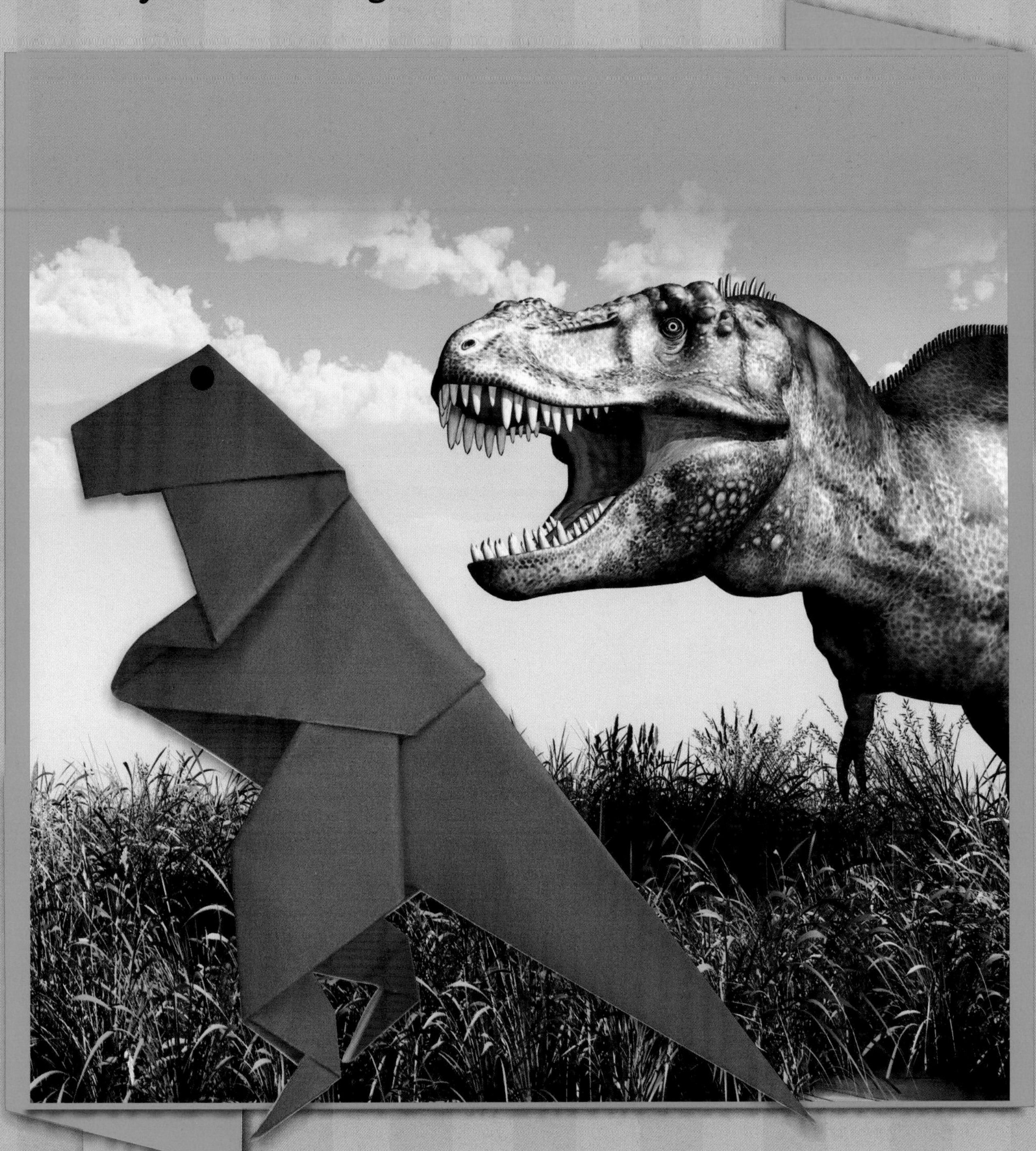

Start with a bird base

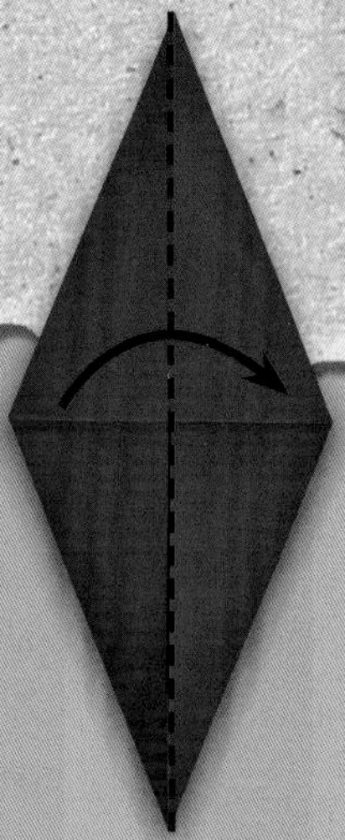

1 Find out how to make a bird base on page 7. Position it so that the flaps with the slit point down. Valley fold the upper flap.

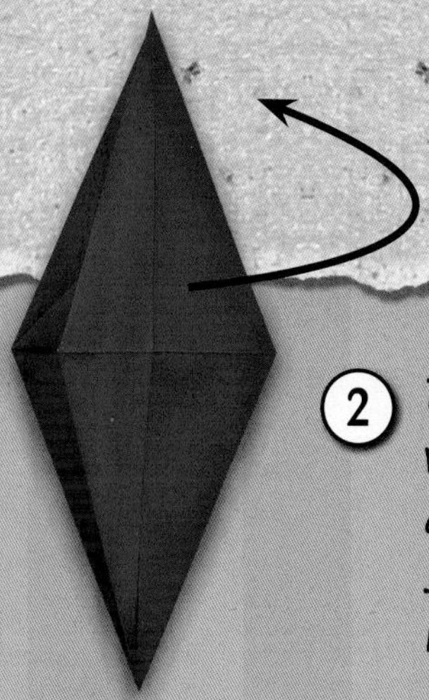

2 Take the right flap at the very back of the paper and swing it to the left, so that two points are revealed at the top, as shown in step 3.

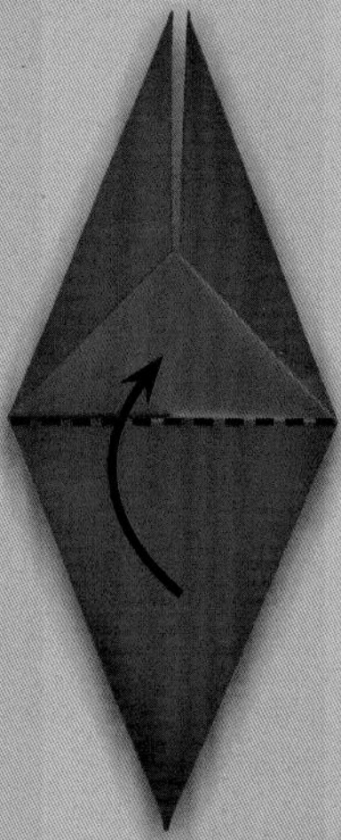

3 Valley fold the bottom flap up to the top.

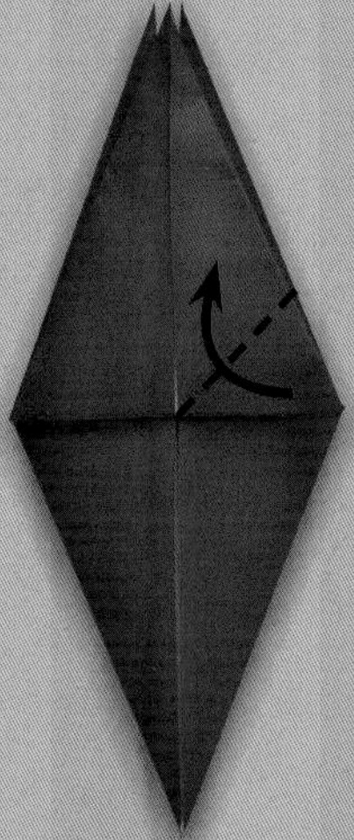

4 Valley fold the bottom corner of the upper right flap into the center.

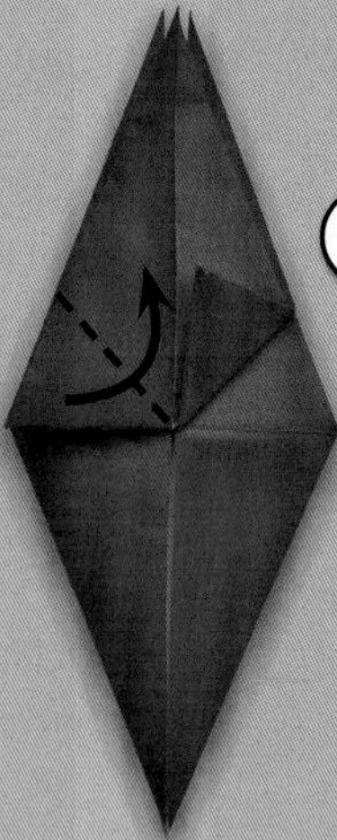

5 Do the same on the other side.

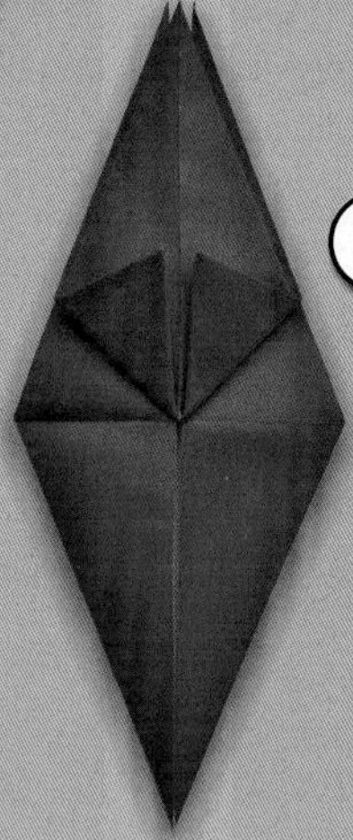

6 The paper should now look like this. Turn the paper over.

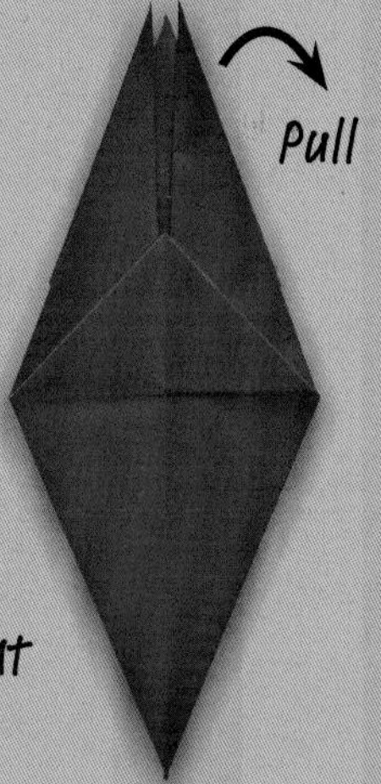

Pull

7 Gently pull out the tall point on the right into the position shown in step 8.

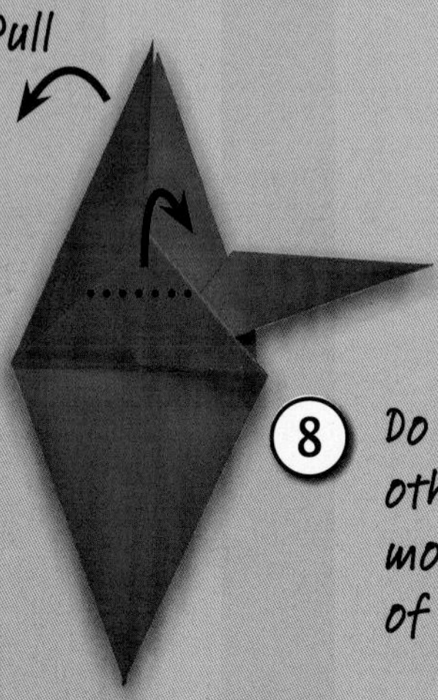

6 Valley fold the bottom section over to the right as shown here.

8 Do the same on the other side. Then mountain fold the tip of the central triangle.

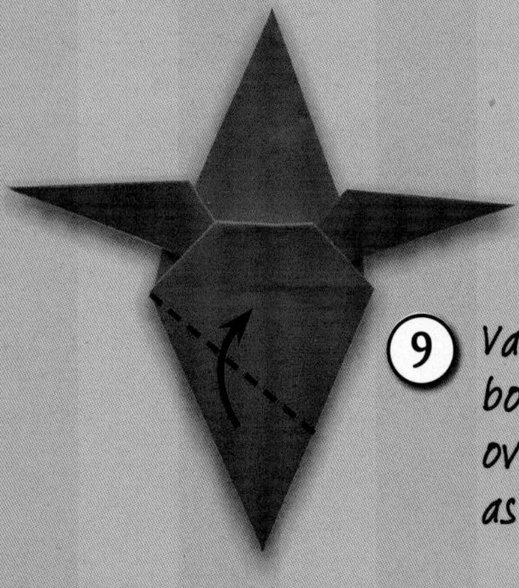

Pull

Did You Know?

Some scientists think that a baby *T. rex* was covered in feathers when it hatched out of an egg.

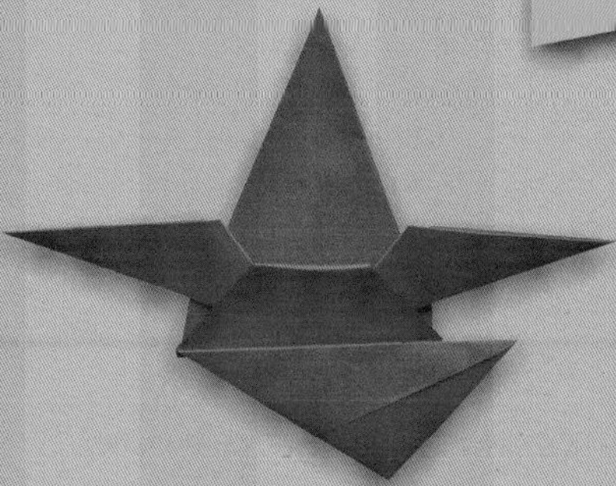

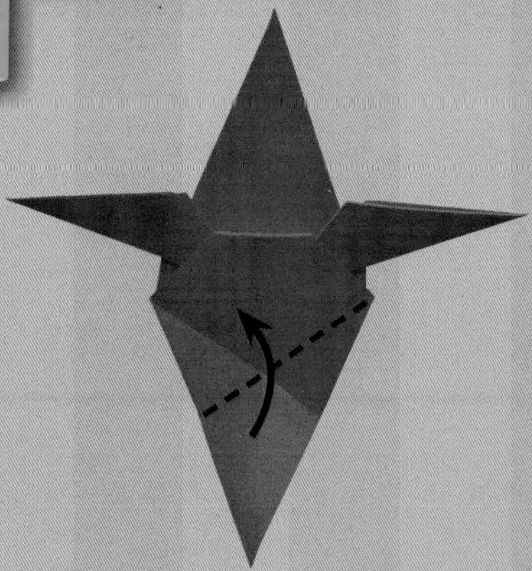

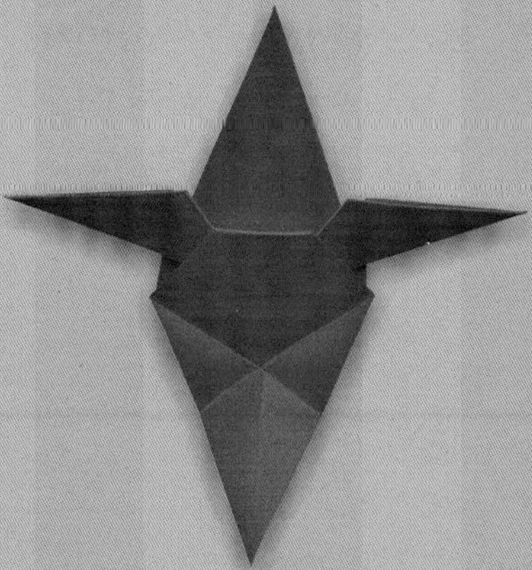

10 The paper should now look like this.

11 Unfold, then valley fold the bottom section over to the left.

12 Unfold, and you should have the crease marks as shown here.

13 Take hold of the left side of the bottom point and push it up and inwards to achieve the shape shown here.

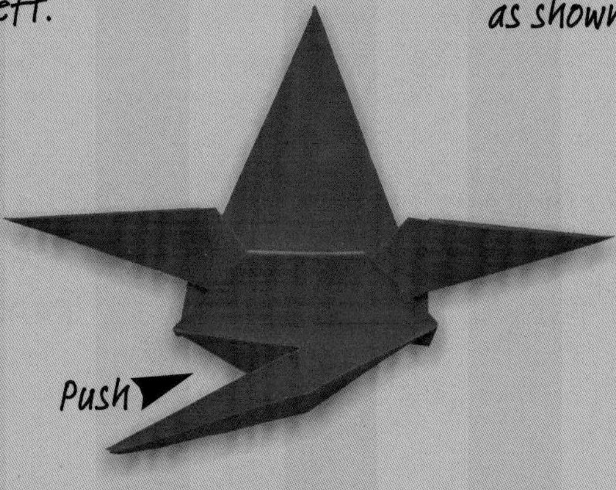

Push▶

14 Flatten the paper to make a triangle at the bottom. Mountain fold the top section, so that the left side folds behind the right.

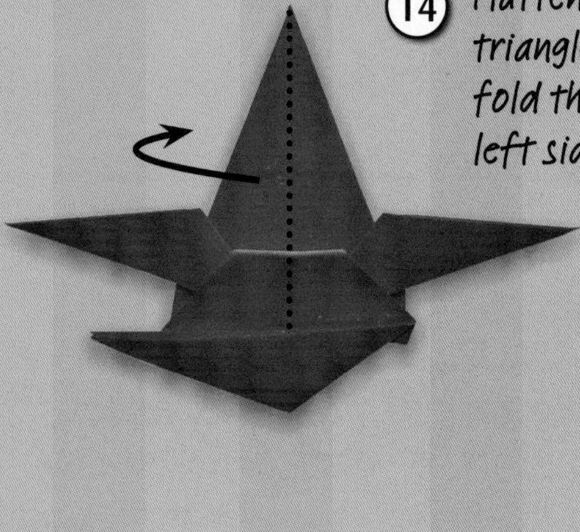

15 The paper should now look like this.

Triangle at top

16 Turn the paper so that the bottom triangle comes up to the top, as shown. Mountain fold the top point.

17 Unfold, then make an outside reverse fold to create the head.

18 Tuck in the tip of the nose to make it blunt.

Push

19 Valley fold where shown. Push down and back on the neck to bring the head down.

20 Mountain fold then valley fold the leg to make a step fold.

21 Unfold the valley fold. Make an inside reverse fold to create the foot. Do the same on the other side.

22 Push the head down a bit more to make it look big and scary. You have created the king of the dinosaurs!

Glossary

base A simple, folded shape that is used as the starting point for many different origami projects.

crease A line in a piece of paper made by folding.

dinosaurs A group of very large reptiles from the Mesozoic Era which are now extinct.

fossil Part of an organism from a past geologic age preserved in Earth's crust.

mountain fold An origami step where a piece of paper is folded so that the crease is pointing upward, like a mountain.

prehistoric From a time before written or recorded history.

step fold A mountain fold and valley fold next to each other.

valley fold An origami step where a piece of paper is folded so that the crease is pointing downward, like a valley.

whip A flexible rod used to strike things with.

Further Reading

Robinson, Nick. *Absolute Beginner's Origami.* New York: Potter Craft, 2006.

Robinson, Nick. *World's Best Origami.* New York: Alpha Books, 2010.

Van Sicklen, Margaret. *Origami on the Go: 40 Paper-Folding Projects for Kids Who Love to Travel.* New York: Workman Publishing Company, 2009.

Index